MAKE HIM AN

OFFER

HE CAN'T

REFUSE

13-Digit ISBN: 978-1-60433-046-5
10-Digit ISBN: 1-60433-046-5

This book may be ordered by mail from the publisher. Please include $2.50 for postage and handling.
Please support your local bookseller first!

Books published by Cider Mill Press Book Publishers are available at special discounts for bulk
purchases in the United States by corporations, institutions, and other organizations. For more
information, please contact the publisher.

Cider Mill Press Book Publishers
"Where good books are ready for press"
12 Port Farm Road
Kennebunkport, Maine 04046

Visit us on the web!
www.cidermillpress.com

Design by Bashan Aquart & Jeff Rogers
Printed in China
1 2 3 4 5 6 7 8 9 0

First Edition

MAKE HIM AN

OFFER

HE CAN'T

REFUSE

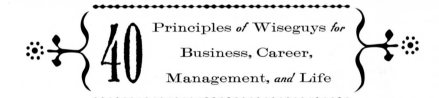

40 Principles *of* Wiseguys *for* Business, Career, Management, *and* Life

by Carlo DeVito

CIDER MILL PRESS BOOK PUBLISHERS

KENNEBUNKPORT, MAINE

CONTENTS

INTRODUCTION

SINCE THE DAWN OF TIME, there have been honest, hardworking people looking to better themselves, their situation, and their community. With each generation, man has hoped to better his lot for his children, and we as a species hope to come to some betterment, taking one more step forward as a group. From this same time, and step-for-step with this same theme, criminals have always been among us.

There have been gangs and bosses since the time of the Roman Empire. Men have seen the holes in the things our society provides or allows and have often used their brilliant minds (and their lack of morals) to provide for the population that which they would outlaw among themselves. The black market has been alive for thousands of years.

And to be fair for just a moment to our ill-behaved brethren, there have been men who amassed huge fortunes using illicit or dishonest means at one time or another—men who were called robber barons. As famed mob boss Meyer Lansky once said about crime and respectability, "Don't worry, don't worry. Look at the Astors and the Vanderbilts, all those big society people. They were the worst thieves—and now look at them. It's just a matter of time." And on the reverse, today we have Kenneth Lay and Dennis Koslowski.

The Modern Mob

They called Prohibition the Great Experiment. If Prohibition accomplished nothing else, it created a Frankenstein monster called organized crime. Vast networks of criminals found opportunities to band together and cooperate in order to provide alcohol to a public yearning for beer and other outlawed spirits. This was the birth of the speakeasy, bootlegging, bathtub gin, and the Thompson machine gun.

It was then that numerous ethnic groups, struggling to create a better way of life, began to sell this contraband. Some criminals liked it. But to others, this new world was too businesslike. Many complained they might has well have gone "legitimate." The Jewish, German, and Irish mobs fought with the Italian mobs. All had their heroes, from Meyer Lansky and Bugsy Segal to Dutch Shultz, Legs Diamond, Al Capone, and Lucky Luciano, and many others.

These men, for better or worse, ran empires, making millions of dollars. They needed to organize their gangs to increase efficiencies and profits, expand distribution, control consumer outlets, and find new sourcing for cheaper production, public's safety be damned. And of course, they did it. They became the stuff of legend.

They were popularized on the big screen by actors like James Cagney, Humphrey Bogart, and George Raft. Eventually they were immortalized in movies like *Once Upon a*

Time In America, *Bugsy*, and the Godfather movies.

Alcohol was eventually legalized, and with it, some members of organized crime went legit, as they say. However, as time moved on, the mob expanded their enterprises into new realms. Prostitution was always a solid earner, as were things like trafficking stolen goods (especially cigarettes, whiskey, and gin). They also sold drugs and committed murder. Hijacking trucks and robbing large deposits of cash were also popular. Drugs eventually came to replace alcohol as organized crime's biggest earner, as portrayed in *Goodfellas*.

This new wave of drug dealing ushered in a new bunch of street entrepreneurs, including Frank Campbell and Nicky Barnes (aka Mr. Untouchable—the toast of the New York tabloid press). The drug era saw the rise of the black and Latino gangsters. These men were more colorful personalities, brash and bold, compared to their older Mafia predecessors—and just as brilliant. The new movies that popularized this group included James Bond films such as *Live and Let Die*, and later films like *American Gangster* and *Carlito's Way*. New immigrant stories surfaced in films like *Scarface*. Gangs and street violence were the bedrock of drug distribution in movies like *Boyz n the Hood* and *New Jack City*.

Eventually, Hollywood came back to the old-fashioned mob in *The Sopranos*, which focused on Tony Soprano and the Italian Mafia in its waning days, straddling the worlds of legitimacy and old-fashioned brutality, while trying to fly under the radar of authorities.

These films and shows have been extremely popular with the general public. Viewers identify with the working-class and hardscrabble heroes they see on the screen, and they're fascinated by these gangsters' struggles for power, wealth, and legitimacy. They get a vicarious thrill from the occasional cinematic rubbing out of a rival or turncoat, since it is well outside of their normal life experience and something they will almost certainly never attempt. There seems to be a never-ending demand for fictional mob shenanigans.

It's Not Personal, It's Business

While the face of organized crime has changed over the decades, in reality each successive wave faces the same challenges that all businesses face. They have to measure their markets, take stock of the competition, and evaluate the strengths and weaknesses of their own organizations. Each has to answer the same inevitable questions: How do I make more money? Where can I expand? Where can I save money? How do I reduce or eliminate competition? How can I create more profit?

Unfortunately, while the women, power, drugs, and guns and knives of the mob world make it look exotic, in fact, each man wakes up thinking about the same thing every other man, legit or otherwise, does: business.

It's always about money, it's always about business. The legitimate, law-abiding businessman shares an ideology with the organized criminal, if not a common language. But the differences are subtle. Take a look at the following lists of terms comparing those used by your typical organized criminal and their counterpart terms in the legit world:

Organized Criminal	Businessman
Talk to our friend	Threaten
Rough up	Demote
Whack	Fire
Cap	Fire
Conquer rival gangs	Mergers and acquisitions
Capo di tutti capo	CEO
Boss	Boss
Captain	Executive
Soldier	Worker
Clocker	Worker
Family	Company
Colors	Company logo

Hit man	Human resources
Consigliere	Consultant
Mouthpiece	Lawyer
Goodfella	Another businessman
Informant	Office rat
Bug	Office IT
Bum	A nonearner
Racket	A particular business
Supply	Goods or services
Cadillac	Success
Piece	Blackberry
Going to the mattresses	All-out war

In *The Godfather*, Kay and Michael are discussing Michael's role in his father's business. Michael tells Kay that his father's business is no different than that of other important men. She asks him if he knows how naive he sounds, but in a sense Michael is right. His father is responsible for many men and their families and the success of an entire operation.

Al Capone—Vicious Mobster or Savvy Businessman?

The best way to equate the business of the mob with that of normal business is to take a look at the real-life case of Al Capone. "Scarface" was a larger-than-life personality who was very important for a number of reasons. For starters, he created the first modern mob. He organized it with bosses and a board of directors who met weekly. This is in fact the same structure that many corporations around the world use to run their companies today. Second, Capone was ostracized by the traditional Mafia, because he was the first criminal to become a large-scale equal opportunity employer. Capone didn't care what your background or ethnicity was. As long as you could perform your job efficiently and profitably, Capone couldn't care less. As a result, the pure Italian Mafia wanted nothing to do with him. Third, Capone ran his business like a business. His reporting structure was by region, and reports were made in total sales and net profits. Fourth and most important, Capone was not caught doing anything illegal for years. He had too many people paid off, too many people involved. He was finally caught when the federal government got hold of his accountant's incredibly detailed business ledgers, which documented all of his earnings—gross and net. The feds got Capone for tax evasion—which, let's be honest, more than a few legitimate businessmen have been guilty of as well. The one overriding thing all businessmen and mobsters should have in common is fear of an audit.

Mob Wisdom for Business Success Today

This book does not advocate or condone illegal or violent acts in the name of business. It does not laud crime or criminals. However, it is meant to bring to light certain business principles that have made less-than-honest men rich—principles that can also be used legally in legitimate business to gain a competitive edge, whatever one's station may be in the business world.

This book highlights wisdom from real-life gangsters and outlaws as well their fictional counterparts. There is no differentiation between the two, since the fictional versions of such men often loom larger in the public's conscience than the real-life, flesh-and-blood inspirations. What wisdom may be gleaned from either, while viewed through the prism of crime and business, is seen as valuable and worth considering as you navigate your way through the mean streets of the business world today.

ALLIANCES

> "The world is changing, and there are new opportunities for those who are ready to join forces with those who are stronger and more experienced."
>
> —"*Lucky*" *Luciano*

PROFILE

Charles "Lucky" Luciano was one of the most successful mob bosses ever. He was known to be tough and ruthless, but he was just as highly respected for his smarts. He was born Salvatore Lucania on November 24, 1897, in Sicily. Luciano is considered the father of modern organized crime and the mastermind of the massive postwar expansion of the international heroin trade. *Time* magazine named Luciano among the twenty most influential builders and titans of the twentieth century.

LESSON

This quote sums up what made Luciano so successful. Like Al Capone, Luciano was willing to work with other crime syndicates to increase influence, power, and distribution. As Luciano points out, for those businessmen willing to view a changing landscape open mindedly, there are always opportunities. The landscape is most likely always changing in your workplace. Is there an alliance that will help build your business, increase your distribution, improve your network of resources? What opportunities are out there that you are not seeing?

AMBITION

"Give me a man who steals a little, and I can make money."

—*Sam Giancana*

PROFILE

Salvatore "Momo" Giancana was born Salvatore Giancana on June 15, 1908. He was a famous Italian-American mobster and boss of the Chicago Outfit from 1956–66. His nicknames included "Momo," "Mooney," "Sam the Cigar," and "Sam Flood." Sam Giancana was arrested more than seventy times in his life yet imprisoned only twice.

LESSON

No businessman likes someone who works for him to steal. But the idea isn't to have dishonest employees. The violent and unpredictable Momo wouldn't have allowed too many hands in the cookie jar. What Giancana is pointing out is that you are always looking for a hungry, ambitious executive who wants to make more. It's important when you find these people to make sure you use them to your advantage. Do you have an underperforming area in your business or your company? Isn't it time you put that young, hungry kid in that spot and see if things shake up a bit? As a manager, you need to let others' ambitions work for you.

17

"He who is deaf, blind, and silent lives a thousand years in peace."

—John Gotti

PROFILE

John Joseph Gotti Jr. was born October 27, 1940, and was commonly known as John Gotti, also nicknamed by the media as the "Dapper Don" and the "Teflon Don." He was a boss of the Gambino crime family, one of the Five Families in New York City. He became widely known for his outspoken personality and flamboyant style that made him the poster child for mobsters, an image that persists even today. Many considered his high-profile media personality a detriment to organized crime. He was convicted of numerous offenses and sentenced to life in prison, where he died.

LESSON

Gotti was ambitious, if nothing else. He had his boss, Paul Castellano, whacked famously in front of Spark Steakhouse in New York City, then he ascended to the throne of New York organized crime. For those who do not take chances, who do not see or hear of opportunities, and who do not speak about advancement, their reward is long life. Gotti's dictum is its unspoken power—those who do not take chances are not rewarded. A life spent in the dark is not worth living. If you want to live your small, dark life forever, Gotti seems to say, *bona fortuna.* But for Gotti himself, such a long, peaceful life would have been death. Is your business life a living death? Are you taking the chances you need to take to advance your career?

"The dream don't come no closer by itself. We gotta run after it now."

—*Carlito "Charlie" Brigante*, Carlito's Way

PROFILE

Carlito "Charlie" Brigante is the antihero/hero of Brian De Palma's 1993 smash-hit movie *Carlito's Way*. It stars Al Pacino as a Puerto-Rican ex-con just released from prison who pledges to stay away from drugs and violence despite the pressure around him, and move on to a better life outside of New York City. It was based on the novel of the same name written by Edwin Torres, who is a judge for the Supreme Court of the State of New York.

LESSON

The ambitious Carlito is talking about seizing an opportunity. He believes that success does not come to us, we must go out and grab it. When it comes near, will we reach out and seize the opportunities that present themselves? Will we see them? Will we run after those opportunities that will help us to realize our dreams? Will we do the extra work needed to advance to the next position? Will we go the extra distance to improve our small business or our major company? "Am I running after the dream, or am I just running?" is the question Carlito seems to be asking us.

ASSOCIATES

> **"In the circle in which I travel, a dumb man is more dangerous than a hundred rats."**
>
> *—Joe Valachi*

PROFILE

Joseph "Joe Cargo" Valachi was born on September 22, 1903. He was the first Mafia member to publicly acknowledge the organization's existence. He is also the person who made *Cosa Nostra* (meaning "this thing of ours") a household name. In October 1963 Valachi, a low-ranking soldier in New York City's powerful Vito Genovese crime family, testified before Arkansas Senator John L. McClellan's congressional committee on organized crime. He testified that the Mafia really did exist. His confessions led to no arrests, but it did provide many details of the Mafia's history, operations, and rituals, and he named many members and the major crime families. Peter Maas eventually wrote Valachi's memoirs, published in 1968 as *The Valachi Papers*, which went on to become a movie starring Charles Bronson as Valachi.

LESSON

Basically Valachi's point is simple: loose lips sink ships. A rat knows what he is trying to accomplish, but a dumb man might say anything. Valachi's wisdom is twofold. One, am I a rat? Am I dumb? One must ask these questions of oneself first. Secondly, do I travel in the company of a rat? Do I travel in the company of one who is dumb? Saying the wrong thing in front of the right people can destroy not only a career but an entire business. It can sabotage everything, even innocently. Choose your associates carefully.

ATTITUDE

"I like to be myself. Misery loves company."

—*Antonio "Tony Ducks" Corallo*

PROFILE

Antonio Corallo was born on February 12, 1913. He became first underboss and then boss of the Gagliano-Lucchese Family in New York. During Corallo's reign, the Lucchese Family positioned itself second under the Gambino organization. He died August 23, 2000.

LESSON

Corallo's corollary is simple—know thyself. Are you a miserable person? Then embrace it. Having a little attitude is not a bad thing, if you can back it up. "Tony Ducks" led the Luchese Family for some thirty years. Could you profit from being a little harder? Are you too nice?

"It really worries the twins what has happened to society since they went down."

—Charles Kray

Charles Kray was an English gangster and the brother of the infamous Kray Twins, Ronnie and Reggie, who were imprisoned for murder in 1969. Ronald and Reginald "Reggie" Kray were identical twin brothers and the foremost organized crime leaders dominating London's East End during the 1950s and 1960s. The Krays were involved in armed robberies, arson, protection rackets, violent assaults involving torture, and the murders of Jack "The Hat" McVitie and George Cornell. As well-dressed West End nightclub owners before their arrests, they mixed with well-known names such as Diana Dors, Frank Sinatra, and Judy Garland as well as prominent politicians. This gave them a perceived respectability, and in the 1960s they became celebrities in their own right, being photographed by the likes of David Bailey and appearing in interviews on television.

LESSON

The passage of time sometimes has a way of changing how we see things. The young grow older, and their world view changes. In their heyday, the Kray Twins were fresh, bright new stars on the international organized crime scene. They were feared, especially for their unique brand of violent torture. Rumors abounded. What's your attitude like? Are you still seeing the world as an opportunity, or are you seeing it as going down? If you see the world as falling off, maybe you better shake up your world view, because time might be passing you by.

"We're not crazed killers. At least I didn't think we were at the time."

—Phillip Leonetti

PROFILE

Phillip "Crazy Phil" Leonetti was born on March 27,1953. He was a Philadelphia gangster who became the underboss of the Philadelphia crime family and eventually a government informant. His criminal record included racketeering charges and ten murders. In 1993 Phillip Leonetti was released from prison after serving only five years.

LESSON

It's all about attitude and perspective. What seems OK now (say, murdering ten people) might in later years seem a little rash. Are you a crazed killer? Are you reckless at work? With other people's careers? The company's position? Office or corporate warfare is sometimes necessary, but are you executing it responsibly? Leonetti apparently was somewhat irresponsible. Sometimes our lives serve as an allegory for others. Is your career going to be an allegory others will retell?

"I gotta hold on to my angst. I preserve it because I need it. It keeps me sharp, on the edge, where I gotta be."

—*Vincent Hanna,* Heat

PROFILE

Vincent Hanna is the hard-working detective played by Al Pacino in the movie *Heat*, opposite Robert De Niro.

LESSON

Hanna's point? You're not going to be successful just walking around with the attitude of a happy-go-lucky business executive or business owner. You need to be on the edge. Like professional athletes, you need to find your edge in the business world as well. You need to constantly be hungry for the next opportunity, always looking for ways to expand distribution, increase profits, everything. You need to keep asking the same questions over and over—how can I be better? How can I make my business better?

BOSSES

**"You don't understand *Cosa Nostra*. Cosa Nostra means
the boss is your boss. Boss is the boss is the boss.
What I'm trying to say is a boss is a boss.
What does a boss mean in this f___in' thing?
You might as well make anybody off the street."**

—Neil Dellacroce

PROFILE

Aniello John Dellacroce was born on March 15, 1914, in Italy. He was also known as "Father Neil," "The Tall Guy," and "The Pollack." He was an Italian immigrant gangster and underboss of the Gambino crime family. Like many Mafia old timers, he shunned attention from the authorities and the public. It was alleged he sometimes dressed like a priest to escape notice.

LESSON

The boss is the boss. Dellacroce couldn't have been any clearer. The chain of command is clear. Don't think it's not. Always keep in mind the chain of command. In our new virtual-office world, e-mail especially blurs the line between your boss and other bosses. Not true. Your boss is your boss. His boss is your boss. But you don't work for his boss—you work for your boss. There is order and structure for a reason. Before you make a major move, always pause and think: is your boss going to like your action? Is his boss going to like your action? And remember, backstabbing your boss (or someone else's) is usually very much frowned upon in the corporate world. Those who get their boss fired or try and pole vault over them are not trusted . . . and usually get fired for trying to do so.

"If you think your boss is stupid, remember: you wouldn't have a job if he was any smarter."

—*John Gotti*

LESSON

Gotti's dictum here is pretty clear. First, your boss is your boss. Second, you wouldn't have a job without him, because he either hired you or at least he didn't whack or fire you. Third and last, with a dumb or lackluster boss, you are freer to take advantage of opportunities and to shine within the organization. A smarter boss might claim your own successes as his own, or might guard your movements too jealously. Don't complain. Earn, shine, enjoy, shut up.

"Look, I'm not stupid. It's the Big Man's wife. I'm gonna sit across from her, chew my food with my mouth closed, laugh at her f---ing jokes, and that's it."

—*Vincent Vega,* Pulp Fiction

PROFILE

John Travolta's Vincent Vega is a semicomatose hit man in Quentin Tarrantino's 1994 organized crime tour de force *Pulp Fiction*. Vega, a homicidal machine who works for L.A. kingpin Marsellus Wallace, is asked to escort the big man's wife, Mia Wallace (played by Uma Thurman), out to a night on the town while Marsellus is elsewhere.

LESSON

The Vega Rule, as it should become known, is unmistakable and irrevocable. You do not flirt or cavort in any way, shape, or form with the Big Man's wife. Not your boss's wife, not his boss's wife. You do not fool around with the spouse of a coworker. Ever. The Vega Rule is the first rule in all of the business world. In the days of the old Mafia, this was an offense to get whacked over—no questions asked. If you touched another Mafia guy's spouse, you were history—no questions asked. It's pretty much the same in business. Don't kid yourself.

CAREER

"You just fulfilled the first rule of law enforcement: make sure when your shift is over you go home alive. Here endeth the lesson."

—Officer Jim Malone, The Untouchables

PROFILE

Sean Connery's hardscrabble Officer Jim Malone, in Brian DePalma's 1987 smash-hit mob flick *The Untouchables*, was a font of organized crime warfare wisdom. As the battle-scarred cop deputized by Kevin Costner's crusading Eliot Ness, he proved to be the inevitable *I Ching* of mob do's and don'ts.

LESSON

Whether you're a police officer, a capo, a cubicle dweller, an executive, or a CEO, your job at the end of the day is to come home alive. Live to fight another day. Sometimes survival is the toughest part. Otherwise you won't be there when the opportunities present themselves. Here endeth the lesson.

"Look out for Number One. If you don't, no one else will."

—Arnold Rothstein

PROFILE

Arnold Rothstein was born January 17, 1882. He was a New York businessman and gambler who became a famous kingpin of organized crime. Rothstein was also widely reputed to have been behind baseball's Black Sox scandal, in which the 1919 World Series was fixed. His notoriety inspired several fictional characters based on his life, including Meyer Wolfsheim in F. Scott Fitzgerald's novel *The Great Gatsby*, and Nathan Detroit in the Damon Runyon story "The Idyll of Miss Sarah Brown," which was made into the musical *Guys and Dolls*.

LESSON

This is one of the cardinal rules of the business world handed down by one of the all-time smartest gangsters in American history. No one else will look out for your interest first. Sure, a mentor might offer advice, but a mentor is also looking out for his own interests. You must think about how everything affects you. Has the company mergered? Are sales up or down? Is demand as sharp or as vigorous as it was? How do each and every one of these things affect you and your business?

"This life of ours, this is a wonderful life. If you can get through life like this and get away with it, hey, that's great. But it's very unpredictable. There's so many ways you can screw it up."

—Paul Castellano

PROFILE

Constantino Paul Castellano was born on June 26, 1915. He was better known as Paul Castellano (or P.C., to his family). He succeeded Carlo Gambino as head of the Gambino crime family, then one of New York's largest Mafia families. In early 1985, he was one of many Mafia bosses arrested on charges of racketeering. While out on bail, Castellano and an associate were shot to death outside Sparks Steak House in Manhattan on the orders of John Gotti, who succeeded him.

LESSON

Castellano had a long, celebrated career before his fall. A career is an obstacle course. You can be the knight in shining armor one month and the bottom of the barrel the next. A successful career is built on hard work, an aggressive nature, and a little luck. Along the way you may win and lose friends. But in the end, you must always be vigilant. No one else will do it for you. You must deal with both success and catastrophe with equal levelheadedness. And you must constantly be thinking about what trip wires may lay ahead. Think about them not as a constant worry but more as the objects in an obstacle field. How will you or your business overcome each obstacle? What's good in the long run?

33

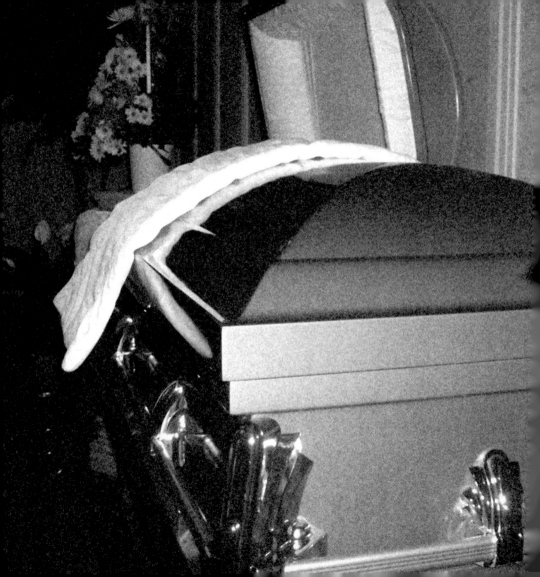

CARELESSNESS

> ## "It's an old habit. I spend my life trying not to be careless. Women and children can afford to be careless, but not men . . ."

—*Don Corleone,* The Godfather

PROFILE

Marlon Brando immortalized the organized crime clan benefactor Don Corleone in Francis Ford Coppola's 1972 masterpiece *The Godfather*. Based on Mario Puzo's bestselling novel, the wise old crime lord/businessman dispensed wisdom almost every time he uttered something. The book and movie were so popular that even future wise guys took their cues from this film on how to act and how to model their organizations and dealings with others.

LESSON

As Don Corleone advised his son Michael with these words, he forcefully reminded us all that we are our own worst enemies. He admonishes his son, but the rule applies just as much to women as it does to men. Carelessness is a dangerous thing. In the office, careless words might sink your own career or someone else's. Sloppy work can result in demotions and firings. In competition between companies, if you are steering the ship, carelessness looms even larger, like an iceberg. Your carelessness will affect others in your company. When making business moves, consider all the angles. How will they affect you personally? Your career? Your company?

CHEATING

"Let him go.
He cheated me fair and square."

—Joseph "Joe Batters" Accardo

PROFILE

Antonino Accardo was born on April 28, 1902. He was also known as "Big Tuna" and "Joe Batters." He was the boss of the Chicago Outfit criminal organization from 1945 to around 1992. Accardo moved The Outfit into new operations and territories, greatly increasing its power and wealth during his tenure as boss.

LESSON

Ever hear of honor among thieves? Yes, there is such a thing. Of course, the scorpion will always be the scorpion, so never trust anyone—or better yet, trust everyone else to be dishonest. Whatever your viewpoint, always assume that the other guy, even the seemingly honest one you are negotiating with, may be taking his own best interests to heart. If you are bested in the office or by a competitor, do not hold a grudge. You must accept responsibility for your own actions. Use your losses, even perceived losses, as lessons. But don't become so paranoid that no one else is allowed to come out with something. Taking all the marbles isn't always the best policy. Allowing someone else a few marbles gives you the ability to do business with them again.

COVER YOUR ASS

"You will put the garbage in the cans and make certain that the cans are covered. We got to keep our own backyard clean."

—*John Gotti*

LESSON

Always make sure you keep your area clean. Not your desk. Your work. Are all the details correct? Is all your paperwork filed? Never give your boss or, in the larger scope, the government, any cause to suspect you. If you are searched or audited, your books need to be in order to avoid problems. Make sure your stuff is together. If it's not, you will pay dearly.

EDUCATION

"Other kids are brought up nice and sent to Harvard and Yale. Me? I was brought up like a mushroom."

—Frank Costello

LESSON

Education is a very important thing. And there can be some mean streets out there if you're not lucky enough to land in a good university. But Costello's complaint is also a badge of honor. While other successful businessmen were sent to such schools, the elegant hoodlum made millions and became famous. His school? Sidewalk University. Just because someone doesn't go to a good school doesn't mean he or she isn't smart. Sometimes the lack of an education or an opportunity makes people hungrier. A sheepskin from a big school might get you in the door, but can you hang with the big boys once you're inside?

ENEMIES

"Never hate your enemies, it affects your judgment."

—*Michael Corleone*, The Godfather II

LESSON

Michael Corleone is talking about vision—your vision of the playing field. Whether you are sizing up the competition in the office or in your industry, you must always keep a clear, cool head. The idea is not to get too emotional. Emotion clouds judgment. Your mind must be free of encumbrances like emotion, so you can concentrate on what your next moves will be and how they will affect yourself, your family, and your company.

ETHICS

"Honest people have no ethics."

—*Sam DeCavalcante*

PROFILE

Simone Rizzo DeCavalcante was born on April 30, 1913. He was known as Sam the Plumber and was a member of the New Jersey Mafia. Claiming descent from the Italian royal family, DeCavalcante was nicknamed "The Count." The Kefauver hearings later named his crime family the DeCavalcante crime family.

LESSON

What DeCavalcante is saying is that people who are honest cannot be compromised.

> **"All my life I've tried to be the good guy, the guy in the white f---ing hat. And for what? For nothing. I'm not becoming like them; I am them."**
>
> —*Joe Pistone*

PROFILE

Joe Pistone was and is a good man. An undercover FBI agent known as Donnie Brasco, he made the right decision and helped to convict a number of organized crime figures. But in the end, many of the men he helped to convict also influenced the way he thought and acted. He had spent so much time undercover that he had become one of them.

LESSON

You may think you are someone who is somehow apart from those with whom you work or who work in your industry. But in the end, how far apart are you?

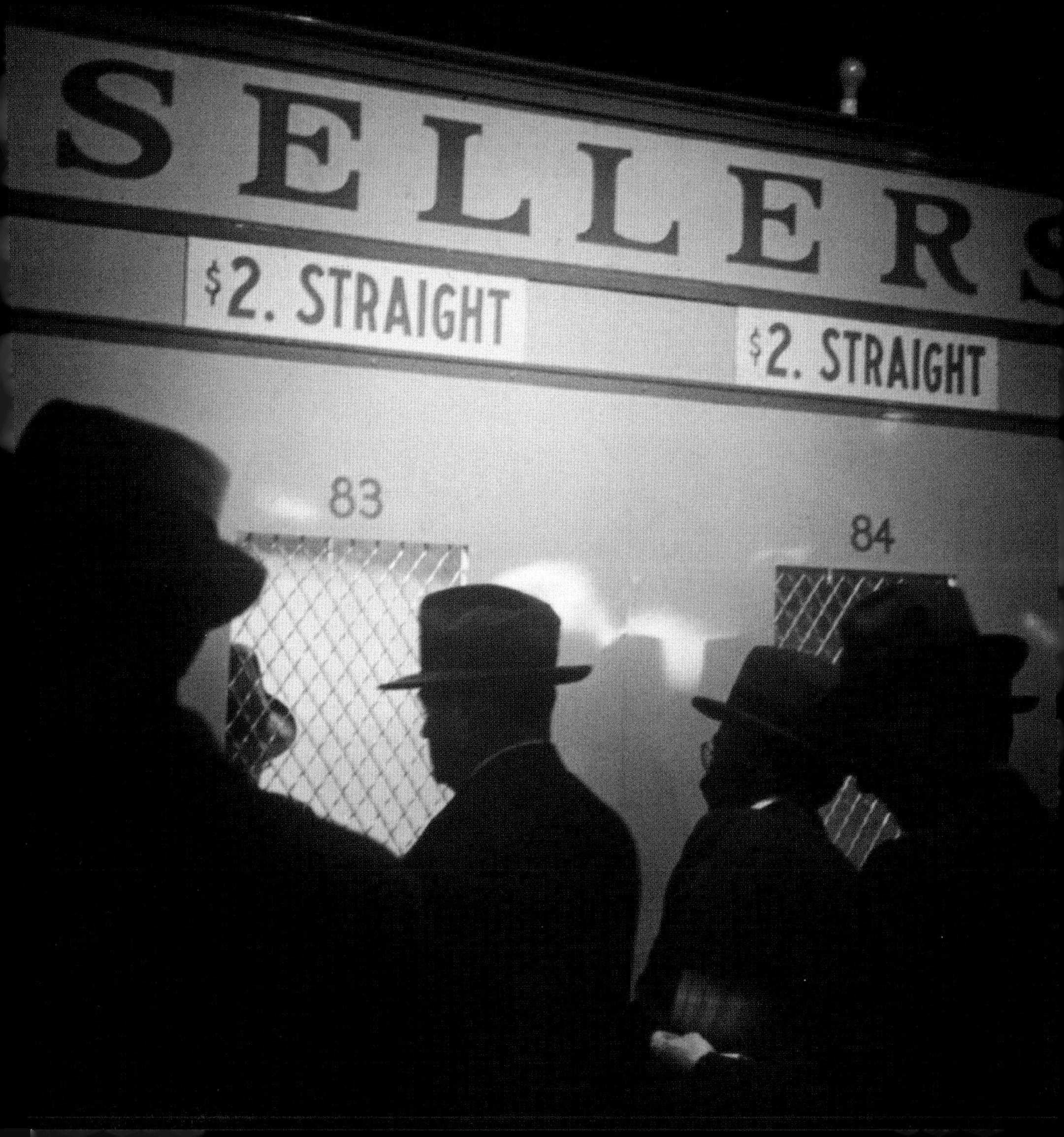
SELLERS
$2. STRAIGHT
$2. STRAIGHT
83
84

FAMILY

"Me, I never had the chance to say,
'Well, I'm going to do something *I* want to do.'
I always did it for my family, for my children,
for my father, for my mother."

—*Thomas Gambino*

PROFILE

Thomas "Tommy" Gambino is an alleged New York mobster and a longtime caporegime of the Gambino crime family. He is the son of family founder Carlo Gambino, the nephew of boss Paul Castellano, and the son-in-law to Lucchese crime family boss Thomas Lucchese.

LESSON

Going to work isn't always about personal satisfaction in life. If it was, everyone would be a rock star, a professional athlete, a movie star, or maybe even a world-famous clothing designer. But we need to remind ourselves that, for many of us, the paycheck is ultimately about family. It's about supporting that family. And it's important to employers as well. Some employers have said they like employees with families and mortgages: they know the pressure is on them to perform. Those workers need the paycheck for more than just themselves.

"Any fool with a dick can make a baby, but only a real man can raise his children."

—*Furious Styles*, Boyz n the Hood

PROFILE

Lawrence Fishburne's Furious Styles was the intellectual voice of reason and responsibility in John Singleton's 1991 blockbuster movie *Boyz n the Hood*, a saga of a group of childhood friends growing up in a Los Angeles ghetto riddled with crime.

LESSON

Parenthood is about responsibility. Being a good parent is important. And being a good mentor at work is also important. Raising a child well helps the child and helps society by extension. Mentoring a young employee helps the employee and the organization. Any idiot can hire an employee, but it takes a responsible manager to help that employee become a productive member of the team—and that reflects well on you!

"A man who doesn't spend time with his family can never be a real man."

—Don Vito Corleone

LESSON

Work is work, and family is family. If you are not willing to be a responsible parent, then how can you be trusted with lives and livelihoods of others within the company where you work? Real adults take on the responsibilities that are theirs. If you cannot face up to your own personal responsibilities for your loved ones, then how can you do the same for your company?

"Natural law. Sons are put on this earth to trouble their fathers."

—*John Rooney*, The Road to Perdition

PROFILE

Paul Newman's John Rooney was a midwestern mob boss in the 2002 Sam Mendes crime drama, *The Road to Perdition*. Set in 1931, the bonds of loyalty are put to the test when a hit man's son witnesses what his father does for a living. Tom Hanks's Michael Sullivan is Rooney's devout gunman until his son witnesses a murder.

LESSON

Being a parent is a tough job. Raising a child isn't easy. As a parent, you never stop hoping that life and all its attendant problems will leave your treasured offspring unharmed. Conversely, being a son or daughter is never easy. Living up to the hopes and expectations of parents can be a tough burden to bear. We all want success for each other. Whether you work together with your family or in separate businesses, the trials and tribulations of your progeny's business and personal fortunes are always a worry.

FEAR

"I never lie, because I don't fear anyone. You only lie when you're afraid."

—*John Gotti*

LESSON

Lying is never good. But it is especially never a good idea to lie out of fear. It almost always gets exposed, and then you look even worse. Fear is a powerful weapon when you use it to your advantage. However, acting out of fear rarely works out well. One must have three-o'clock-in-the-morning courage. You must be able to detach yourself from your situation and use clear, cold logic.

"Testa would later tell Caramandi, 'Now we can kill guys without bullets. They use their own guns. That's how afraid they are of us.'"

—Salvatore Testa

PROFILE

Salvatore Testa was a boss in the Scarfo Philadelphia crime scene. Testa said this to a Scarfo gunman after Enrico Riccobene (son of a mobster), who had no real connection to a Philly mob war, committed suicide. According to crime historian Allan May, "While working at his jewelry store on December 14, 1983, he was notified that Testa, Phil Leonetti, and Lawrence Merlino were looking for him. Enrico went to the safe, pulled out a gun, and shot himself in the head."

LESSON

Fear is a powerful ally. In business as in the mob, there are people who will take themselves out of the picture due to fear—perceived loss of prestige, an impending job loss, unhappiness in their current working environment. Fear makes people do things they might not otherwise do.

FIRINGS

"**When they send for you, you go in alive, you come out dead, and it's your best friend that does it.**"

—*Lefty Ruggiero*

PROFILE

Benjamin "Lefty" Ruggiero was a member of the Bonanno crime family and a close friend/soldier under Dominic "Sonny Black" Napolitano. His story is told in Joe Pistone's book and movie *Donnie Brasco*.

LESSON

In the business world, when you get called into your boss's office and the human resources person is there, it's rarely good. If you're a marked man, no one's going to tell you. Probably not even your best friend will tell you when you're marked. If your boss has stopped returning your e-mails and friends in the company seem to be opting out of having lunch with you, then you're probably going to have one of those meetings soon.

"Can't anybody shoot that guy so he won't bounce back up?"

—Dutch Schultz, about Jack "Legs" Diamond

PROFILE

Dutch Schultz (August 6, 1902–October 24, 1935) was a New York City–area gangster of the 1920s and 1930s. Born Arthur Flegenheimer in the Yorkville section of Manhattan, he made his fortune in organized crime–related activities such as bootlegging and the numbers racket. At the time of his death, Schultz was estimated be worth more than seven million dollars.

LESSON

If you have to give someone a warning at work, make it once and make it clear. Don't keep giving warnings. Eventually, if they can't or won't do the job they were hired to do, they have to be fired. Not dismissing an unsatisfactory employee promptly leads people to question your judgment, ability, and leadership.

"I never killed a guy who didn't deserve it."

—Mickey Cohen

PROFILE

Meyer Harris "Mickey" Cohen was a gangster based in Los Angeles from the 1930s through the 1970s. Cohen went from Brooklyn to Manhattan to working for The Outfit in Chicago before making his move out West. His list of associates included Bugsy Seigel and Meyer Lansky, and he was supposedly a good friend of William Randolph Hearst.

LESSON

People get fired. Sometimes they deserve it, and sometimes they're simply in the wrong place at the wrong time. The company doesn't owe you a job. Whether you've been working for the company for fifteen minutes or for twenty years, if you are not continually evolving and morphing into someone who produces, you are becoming unnecessary overhead. There is always someone ready to take your job. You took someone else's job, and someday someone else will take yours. The one thing you know when they make you head coach of any sports team is that one day you will be fired. And mob guys know, few of them end up in retirement homes.

"Murders came with smiles, shooting people was no big deal for us goodfellas."

—*Henry Hill*, Goodfellas

LESSON

People get fired. It's part of business. Some people you're happy to fire—they've been disruptive, disobedient, perhaps fomenting unhappiness. Other people you hate to fire: the guy who tried hard but couldn't cut it; a person who's worked for the company for a long time but is not willing to adapt to new ideas and procedures as the company grows. Firing people is part of the job. You have to make the decisions you feel are in the best interest of the company. You can't hold back. And when you do it, do it nicely, no matter your personal feelings. Be professional.

"If you're clipping someone, I always say, make sure you clip the people around him first. Get them together, 'cause everybody's got a friend. He could be the dirtiest [expletive] in the world, but someone that likes this guy, that's the guy that sneaks you."

—*Ilario Zannino*

PROFILE

Ilario "Larry Biona" Zannino was the muscle and head gambling honcho for Raymond J. Patriarca and the Patriarca crime family. Zannino was one of the richest gangsters in the New England mob. The *Boston Globe* stated that Zannino has a wallet that looks like the inside of the New England Merchants Bank vault, and a bookmaking and loan-sharking operation more successful than most American car companies.

LESSON

Patchwork responses to problems at work are not solutions. You have one or two people fomenting disharmony on your team, you have to cut them out quick. When you have someone spreading unhappiness, it spreads fast and furious. You have to be quick, decisive and ruthless. If you let the person and their hangers-on linger, they will continue to spread their version of things, and make office life unbearable. Cut off the head, and confront the rest. If you don't, they will come gunning for *you*.

"You can imagine my embarrassment when I killed the wrong guy."

—*Joe Valachi*

LESSON

Looking to assign culpability in the workplace isn't always accurate or productive. People make mistakes. However, people who keep making mistakes need to be whacked. Make sure, though, when you blow your stack or fire someone, you've got the right person. Are they the problem—or the patsy?

"We only kill each other."

—Benjamin "Bugsy" Siegel

PROFILE

Benjamin "Bugsy" Siegel (February 28, 1906–June 20, 1947) was an American gangster who was behind the large-scale development of Las Vegas. His associates included Meyer Lansky, Mickey Cohen, and numerous other mobsters, as well as Hollywood actors like George Raft. Seigel was known to be quick with a gun in his early years and prone to violence.

LESSON

People of a kind tend to fight with each other. While healthy competition can engender hard work between groups, managers pitted against each other may breed anger and resentment throughout departments and entire organizations. If this happens, things can deteriorate rapidly from a healthy environment to a street war. As a manager, make sure you never get caught pitting people inappropriately against one another, and don't let your rivalries in the workplace get out of hand.

"You live by the gun and knife and die by the gun and knife."

—*Joe Valachi*

LESSON

Each of us has a tool that we use. If you are successful, you may use that tool over and over. But someone else, usually a competitor, will always find a way to adapt that tool (a discount, a rebate, a promotion, delayed billing), and may even improve upon it. If you do not develop enough tools and constantly improve your tools as time goes by, your tools will become obsolete, and so will you. If your work strategy is always to do x and it succeeds, you can be sure others around you will notice and also start doing it. How will you respond?

"Sit your five-dollar ass down before I make change."

—Nino Brown, New Jack City

PROFILE

Mario Van Peebles's 1991 blockbuster crime thriller *New Jack City* is a modern-day crime epic set amidst the height of New York City's crack cocaine epidemic of the late 1980s and early 1990s. At the film's center is Nino Brown, the head of a vast crack cocaine empire.

LESSON

Veiled threats in the workplace are sometimes unavoidable. And sometimes that's not a bad thing. People genuinely like order and strong direction. That does not mean you should be hollering at employees and always walking around beating your chest. A rare but solid display of power though can sometimes mean the difference between a well-established chain of command and cubicle anarchy.

FORGET ABOUT IT

What's "forget about it"?

—FBI technician

Donnie Brasco: "Forget about it" is like if you agree with someone—you know, like "Raquel Welch is one great piece of ass, forget about it." But then, if you disagree, like "A Lincoln is better than a Cadillac? Forget about it!" you know? But then, it's also like if something's the greatest thing in the world, like *mangia* those peppers, "forget about it." But it's also like saying "Go to hell!" too. Like, you know, like "Hey Paulie, you got a one-inch pecker," and Paulie says "Forget about it!" Sometimes it just means forget about it.

LESSON

Sometimes it's better to say too little than too much. "Forget about it" is one of those phrases that allows mobsters to respond without really saying anything. Try it at work sometime—at the very least, you should get a few laughs!

FRIENDSHIP

"**Mafia is a process, not a thing. Mafia is a form of clan-cooperation to which its individual members pledge lifelong loyalty. . . . Friendship, connections, family ties, trust, loyalty, obedience—this was the glue that held us together.**"

—*Joseph Bonanno*

PROFILE

Giuseppe "Joseph/Joe" Bonanno was a Sicilian-born American mafioso who became the boss of one of the infamous Five Families of New York City. He was one of the longest-living dons in American Mafia history. He eventually retired after a heart attack and moved to Arizona, where he lived out the rest of his life and wrote *A Man of Honor,* a national bestselling autobiography.

LESSON

No company expects your loyalty akin to that of your family, your religion, or your nation. But being on the team is a big thing. To have a successful business, everyone on your staff, down to the lowest person, needs to believe in your company and its products or services. If they don't, why do you have them there? If you don't believe, why are you there? Understand the strengths and weaknesses of your organization and take them to heart. That way everyone is on the same page and pointed in the same direction instead of pulling in different directions or, worse, sowing seeds of discontent within the organization.

GOSSIP

"No bum talks about a bum."

—Carlo Gambino

PROFILE

Carlo "Don Carlo" Gambino was born on August 24, 1902. He was the founder of the Gambino crime family. No one expected Gambino to seize control over the Commission of Cosa Nostra in the United States at the 1957 Apalachin convention. Gambino was known for being low-key and secretive, and unlike many modern mafiosi, Gambino served relatively little time in prison. He lived to the age of seventy-four, then on October 15, 1976, he died of a heart attack while watching the New York Yankees on television. Gambino lived his life well beneath the radar of the media and the law. He was incredibly secretive and lived a simple, not very exotic life. However, he controlled the workers in the Garment District and remained quite powerful throughout his life.

LESSON

Gambino's point here is that people who bad-mouth other people are often not well thought of themselves. This certainly holds true in the workplace. Shun gossip like it's a plague.

"Never open your mouth unless you're in the dentist chair."

—Sammy "The Bull" Gravano

LESSON

Here's a case of "Do as I say and not as I do." Gravano's code of silence, as espoused here, is the classic mobster's stance. However, it must be pointed out that Gravano himself turned out to be one of the biggest stool pigeons (thankfully for law enforcement officials) in U.S. mob history. To this day, his boss, John Gotti, is still idolized and mimicked by up-and-comers, while Gravano is seen as a bum.

"Don't let your tongue be your worst enemy."

—"Sonny" Franzese

PROFILE

The New York–based Colombo/Persico/Orena family of La Cosa Nostra has approximately 120 members as well as more than 450 associates. One faction based in New York and allegedly headed by capo John "Sonny" Franzese has become particularly well known for its fraudulent activities. He has served four federal prison sentences.

LESSON

People who talk too much make enemies faster than they make friends. If you talk often and long enough around the office, your mouth will eventually get you in trouble.

HONOR

"There are certain promises you make that are more sacred than anything that happens in a court of law, I don't care how many Bibles you put your hand on. Some of the promises, it's true, you make too young, before you really have an understanding of what they mean. But once you've made those first promises, other promises are called for. And the thing is, you can't deny the new ones without betraying the old ones. The promises get bigger, there are more people to be hurt and disappointed if you don't live up to them. Then, at some point, you're called upon to make a promise to a dying man."

—*Paul Castellano*

LESSON

You want to be a good as your word. Honor those whom you should honor. But never make a promise. Business is business. People who want to extract promises are those who cannot help themselves in some way, shape, or form. They want you to do their heavy lifting because they themselves cannot—especially in business. That's why contracts were created. A promise will always compromise you. Steer clear of people who want promises. Neither should you ask for promises that may compromise someone else.

"When I think of the American Indian, I think of their courage, strength, pride, their respect and loyalty toward their brothers. I honor the reverence they share for tradition and life. These traits are hungered for in a society that is unfortunately plagued by those whose only values are self-centered and directed at others' expense . . ."

—John Gotti

PROFILE

For all his bravado and high living, which eventually brought heat on himself and the family that he led, Gotti was someone very popular with the rank-and-file mobsters. He was very well thought of by them. He deposed Paul Castellano because he thought Castellano had forgotten his brethren-in-crime while he lived in his mansion on Todd Hill, Staten Island.

LESSON

Business throws a wide variety of people together. You must be yourself in business. Don't get caught up in who everyone else is. Try to keep in mind your center of being: where you came from and who you are. Gotti was well-loved by his underlings, not for his bravado or tailored suits but because he did not forget the men in the streets from which he came (unlike his predecessor Paul Castellano, who lived in the suburbs in a mansion and lost touch with his rank-and-file "soldiers").

"**All I have in this world is my balls and my word,
and I don't break them for no one.**"

—*Tony Montana,* Scarface

**If you give someone your word in business, it's important to keep
that word. It's gettin' so a businessman can't expect no return from
a fixed fight. Now, if you can't trust a fix, what can you trust?**"

—*Johnny Caspar,* Miller's Crossing

PROFILE

Miller's Crossing was judged one of the 100 greatest films ever made. The film is set during the Prohibition era in an unnamed northeastern U.S. city, where two warring gangs face off. Caught between the two sides is Tom Reagan, an ambivalent, enigmatic protagonist who may or may not be plotting against his boss. Leo O'Bannon, a headstrong Irishman, controls the town, but his power is in danger of being usurped by a rival gang headed by the ambitiously violent Italian, Giovanni Gasparo, aka Johnny Caspar.

LESSON

Sometimes corruption is a reliable thing. But the real meaning of Caspar's lament is that there is no such thing as a "sure thing." Anyone who believes that there is will soon be double-crossed. As the saying goes, a fool and his money are soon parted. Don't be a fool. Don't follow a "sure thing." The only sure things in business are death, taxes, and the good, old-fashioned double-cross.

LAW

"A lawyer with a briefcase can steal more than a thousand men with guns."

—*Don Vito Corleone*

LESSON

Sometimes the biggest crooks are not those of organized crime. Sometimes they are businessmen who embezzle, and sometimes they are corporations that are just smart enough to make a big killing while skirting the law at the same time.

"Goodfellas don't sue goodfellas. Goodfellas kill goodfellas."

—Salvatore Profaci

PROFILE

Alledged Colombo family caporegime Salvatore Profaci is the son of Joseph "Joe the Boss" Profaci, who was the original family head before Joe Colombo. His sister Rosalie is married to Salvatore "Bill" Bonanno, son of Joseph Bonanno. Salvatore was convicted of mail fraud in December 1985 and sentenced to four years in federal prison.

LESSON

This really is a street version of Machiavelli's famed line: "Never do an enemy a small injury." The law in the mob world is that you don't take another goodfella to court. You take him out. If a sit-down doesn't work for you, then you need to make something happen otherwise. The law is either kill or be killed. Make sure you think about all the angles when you are looking to take someone out.

"According to my best recollection, I don't remember."

—Vincent "Jimmy Blue Eyes" Alo

PROFILE

Born in Manhattan, Alo began working on Wall Street at age fourteen. As a young man, Alo was convicted of armed robbery and sent to state prison. In 1926, Alo became a made man in Joseph "Joe the Boss" Masseria's powerful New York gang. In 1929, Alo was introduced to Meyer Lansky by Lucky Luciano, and the two became fast and lifelong friends.

LESSON

A bad memory in the face of inquisition has saved many a man. The old amnesia routine is the famous rope-a-dope of the mob world. As any law enforcement professional will tell you, if there is one thing most wise guys have, it's good, long memories. This ploy has been used very successfully by many business executives and high ranking government officials also claiming foggy memories when called upon to testify in a court of law.

" 'The United States of America versus Anthony Spilotro.' Now what kind of odds are those?"

—Tony "The Ant" Spilotro

PROFILE

Anthony "Tony the Ant" Spilotro (May 19, 1938–June 14, 1986) was a small, infamous, Italian-American mobster and enforcer for the Chicago Outfit in Las Vegas during the 1970s and 1980s. As portrayed in the movie *Casino*, directed by Martin Scorcese, Spilotro's job was to protect and oversee the Outfit's illegal casino profits, called "the skim." Spilotro's violent temper and out-of-control lifestyle eventually left him on the wrong end of a baseball bat in a cornfield in Indiana. His fictionalized name in the movie was Nicky Santoro.

LESSON

When a prosecutor has you in his sights, you become a dead man walking. Even if you beat the prosecutor's office once, they'll come back at you again, guaranteed. The real lesson here is: don't fool around with the law. And if they don't get you, one of your own guys (your boss?) will. Spilotro went to jail several times, but when he became an embarrassment to the mob, they had him whacked. So, if you get into legal trouble at work, your company will do whatever it has to do to distance itself from you. The odds for you in such situations simply aren't good.

"We're not children here. The law is—how should I put it? A convenience. Or a convenience for some people and an inconvenience for other people."

—*Paul Castellano*

LESSON

Once the federal government is on to you, your days are numbered. End of story. Few wise guys have beaten federal prosecutors in court—especially in a court of law, with so many people at their disposal, the prosecutors can be ruthless. Better start making arrangements once the feds have you in their sights—businessman or mobster.

LOYALTY

"Shoot me. But I'm not going to answer any questions."

—*Venero "Benny Eggs" Mangano*

PROFILE

Venero Frank "Benny Eggs" Mangano was born September 7, 1921, and was allegedly a high-ranking member of the Genovese crime family. The nickname "Benny Eggs" came from his mother running an egg farm. He was released from prison on November 2, 2006, after serving a fifteen-year sentence for extortion.

LESSON

Mangano's vow of silence is an important one. In business, a big mouth can be a detriment. However, Mangano's quote isn't here for this bit of wisdom. It's included because he was willing to be shot rather than give up information about his business. What manager wouldn't want a man like that working for him? That's loyalty.

LYING

"Don't lie. Tell one lie, then you gotta tell another lie to compound on the first."

—*Meyer Lansky*

LESSON

It can't be put any more plainly or simply: *don't lie*. It always comes back to bite you, and then you look even more untrustworthy. And your misdeeds will follow you as well. Other employees will remember and relate it to others. If you screw up at work, understand how you erred. Then explain that you have a solution to the problem you have created and that you will take steps not to let it happen again. Do this, or else start polishing your resume. Don't lie at work, no matter what.

"I always tell the truth. Even when I lie."

—*Tony Montana*, Scarface

LESSON

Always tell the truth. *Always.* A lie will always be found out, and then you are really in trouble, not just now, but most likely for a long time to come.

MANAGEMENT

> ❝In Bensonhurst, that was it, becomin'
> a made guy. It's all we kids ever talked
> about. . . . I never saw the other side of it
> until I was in, and then it's too late and
> you just do your work . . . ❞
>
> —Sammy "The Bull" Gravano

LESSON

You may dream of becoming someone big and important at work—a vice president, a CEO, an owner—but know that those guys deal with nothing but problems all day long. It's not as cool as it looks. It's hard and the pressure is always on. Someone makes a mistake? How are you going to rectify it? Sales down? How are you going to get them up? Newest product launch dies? What's the next newest thing? Being a manager has its multitude of drawbacks. Look at the lion. Once he takes over a pride, most of his time is spent marking his territory and fighting off hyenas and other male lions, until one day he is deposed or killed by rivals. Being a manager is a lot like being a male lion: it has its glory moments, but a lot of it is just hard work under pressure.

"You a gangster now. You can't learn it at school . . . you can't have a late start."

—*Carlito,* Carlito's Way

LESSON

Being a mobster isn't something that just anyone can do. One has to learn the rules, customs, and angles by playing the game. While many mobsters are not book-smart, they are aggressive and street-smart. No matter what business you enter, you're going to have to be able to hit the ground running. No one's out to do you any favors. Make sure you know what you're getting yourself into and that you're smart and strong enough to play the game.

"**For a second, I thought I was dead, but when I heard all the noise I knew they were cops. Only cops talk that way. If they had been wise guys, I wouldn't have heard a thing. I would've been dead.**"

—*Henry Hill*, Goodfellas

LESSON

In truth, as a manager you rarely see the end coming. You are always the last to know. Your friends will suspect. They may even know. Others certainly will. It's only a matter of when. The only difference between a job and the mob is two weeks' severance.

"Let's take a son-in-law, somebody, put them into the [union] office; they got a job. Let's take somebody's daughter, whatever, she's the secretary.
Let's staff it with our people . . . And when we say go break this guy's balls . . . they're there, seven o'clock in the morning to break the guy's balls."

—Anthony "Tony Ducks" Corallo

PROFILE

Corallo grew up in an Italian section of East Harlem. He got his nickname "Tony Ducks" by ducking prosecutions. He was successful at extortion, bookmaking, gambling, etc. He eventually became a boss in the Luchese crime family. Corallo would eventually become a victim of the RICO Act. He was convicted and sentenced to one hundred years in prison. In 2000, Anthony Corallo died at a medical center for federal prisoners.

LESSON

Who are you trying to manage? Are you managing the people who work for you? Or are you managing someone else? Sometimes one of the smart ways to manage people is to have other people manage them for you. Managing isn't about telling someone what to do. That's small thinking. Sometimes it's getting someone to do something for you by getting other people to help you.

"I called your f------ house five times yesterday, now, if you're going to disregard my m----- f------ phone calls, I'll blow you and that f ------ house up . . . This is not a f------ game. My time is valuable. If I ever hear anybody else calls you and you respond within five days, I'll f------ kill you."

—*John Gotti*

LESSON

Every once in a while, a stern scolding of a business underling is an important tool of management. While the old-fashioned expletive is strongly discouraged in the cubicles of modern business, laying down the law is always a good idea. It does one of two things: 1) it lets that person know they will not get away with noncompliance; or 2) they will decide they don't want to put up with you, in which case, your problem is solved anyway.

"Am I my brother's keeper? Yes I am."

—*Nino Brown,* New Jack City

LESSON

Managing people is all about being their keeper, whether they like to admit it or not. Are you their babysitter? No. Are you there to keep them focused and on message? Yes. As a manager, you are judged on how well people beneath you perform. A bad performance by a worker beneath you is a bad reflection on you. Maybe you need to be a strong leader. Maybe only a light touch is required. But you are a keeper of sorts.

"I don't like violence, Tom. I'm a businessman. Blood is a big expense."

—*Virgil Solozzo,* The Godfather

LESSON

Knocking off people is tough and expensive. It's not a great way to do business. Doing business is the best way to make money. Fighting costs you time and energy. Think before you want to go to war with someone—What does it win you? What does it cost you? Who will you alienate? How will the new lay of the land benefit you? What will the negatives of the new layout (and there are always negatives) be?

"For most of the guys, killing's got to be accepted. Murder was the only way that everybody stayed in line. You got out of line, you got whacked. Everybody knew the rules. But sometimes, even if people didn't get out of line, they got whacked."

—*Henry Hill*

LESSON

Order is order. There need to be some rules—even in the mob. Rules are there to keep people in line.

MARKETING

"When I sell liquor, it's called bootlegging; when my patrons serve it on Lake Shore Drive, its called hospitality."

—*Al Capone*

LESSON

Business is all about marketing. What's undesirable to some may be heaven to others.

> **"In the casino, the cardinal rule is to keep them playing and to keep them coming back. The longer they play, the more they lose, and in the end, we get it all."**
>
> —*Ace Rothstein,* Casino

PROFILE

Ace Rothstein was the fictional character based on Frank Lawrence "Lefty" Rosenthal. Swedish-American by birth, he was adopted by a west side Jewish family in Chicago. It was there he developed a close friendship with known Outfit enforcer Anthony Spilotro. He had numerous arrests and indictments for gambling crimes, including bribing players to fix football, basketball, and other games. He was never convicted.

LESSON

How many ways can you keep your customer coming back for more? Are you doing everything you can to enhance their experience? Are you doing everything you can to make sure they want to buy your next product or service? What can you do to make it better? There is always something—always—and you've got to find out what it is.

MISTAKES

> ## "I know where my mistakes are, where I made my mistakes. They're too late to remedy, you know what I mean?"
>
> —*John Gotti*

LESSON

This is the mobster's version of "don't cry over spilt milk." In other words, don't dwell on your mistakes at work. Come up with solutions to your problems, and when it comes time, face up to your mistakes. Own them. Don't slough them off on someone else. If you made sound decisions, and it just didn't work, that happpens all the time in business. If you made foolish decisions, own up to them. There is no respect in the business world for someone who doesn't own up to his mistakes.

MONEY

"Money talks, and bullshit runs a marathon."

—*Nino Brown*

LESSON

In business, money is king. If you don't have the money to do what you want to do in business, you'll need to work a lot harder. There's no short way around it. If you have a great idea and no capital to back it up, then it's not worth anything yet. You have to find financing—a loan, a backer, investors. Your path may ultimately coincide with the guys who have money, but your road is going to be a little longer.

"There's no such thing as good money or bad money. There's just money."

—Charlie "Lucky" Luciano

LESSON

There's old money, and there's new money; there's clean money and dirty money. But in business, let's face it: money is money. You either have it or you don't. You can afford something or you can't. Many people who make lots of money in business do so to live a higher lifestyle, and there's nothing wrong with that. Don't ever apologize or feel ashamed for how you made your money.

"Behind every great fortune, there is a crime!"

—Charlie "Lucky" Luciano

LESSON

Luciano's hypothesis is a skeptical one. But in the end, he is talking not just about crimes but also about malfeasance. Many of the world's great business fortunes have been built on the backs of other's misfortunes, mistakes, or hard work. Some companies have taken advantage of poor legislation that favored them, which in retrospect seems unjust. Sometimes they have used their power to dominate the marketplace until the world catches up to them. In business, things are seldom completely on the up and up.

> **"Don't worry, don't worry. Look at the Astors and the Vanderbilts, all those big society people. They were the worst thieves, and now look at them. It's just a matter of time."**
>
> —*Meyer Lansky*

LESSON

Indeed some misdeeds were committed by the Astors, the Vanderbilts, and other well-known families of business who built great fortunes. Many past abuses may be attached to their business dealings. But through the wash of time, their family names have been laundered (often through philanthropy) to restore their lustrous images in the eyes of the adoring and unwitting public.

> **"Always overpay your taxes. That way you'll get a refund."**
>
> —*Meyer Lansky*

LESSON

Lansky's point is simple. The way all greedy mobsters and businessmen get caught in the end is by taxes. It's one of the two inescapable facts of life (death, of course, being the other). Don't prove yourself to be an idiot. Give unto Caesar before Caesar takes what's his (and throws you in jail, to boot).

NEGOTIATION

> ❝You can get much further with a kind word and a gun than you can with a kind word alone.❞
>
> —*Al Capone*

LESSON

A kind word always helps in business negotiations. A pat on the back, a shake of the hands. But when push comes to shove, a nice word and something to back it up are always a good trump card. Sometimes force is necessary in business—not physical, but some sort of a show of power. "Muscle" of this sort can play an important role in your business negotiations. It's knowing how and when to use it that will get you ahead—or get you into trouble.

"They pull a knife, you pull a gun. He sends one of yours to the hospital, you send one of his to the morgue. That's the Chicago way!"

—*James Malone,* The Untouchables

PROFILE

The Brian DePalma version of Elliott Ness's cleaning up of Chicago in *The Untouchables* features the tough police officer named James Malone who helps Ness, a federal agent, understand the rules of the street in his fight against Al Capone.

LESSON

When you do business with people who play rough, you need to hold your ground and be able to shove back. Usually the biggest bully in business, just like in the schoolyard, is also the biggest baby. A good counterattack is always a great remedy. Don't let people at work push you around. Fight back. Speak up. No one else will necessarily stand up for you. You have to fight your own battles or accept defeat. Unfortunately, confrontation is often part of the everyday business world. Be ready to deal with it.

"Ever since we was kids, we always knew that people can be bought. It was only a question of who did the buyin' and for how much."

—Charlie "Lucky" Luciano

LESSON

Everyone in business has a price. For many people its money. For others the prize may be something else—a nice lunch or an expensive dinner, perhaps a hunting or fishing trip or a trip for two to some romantic locale. Whatever you want comes with a price. But what is that price? And what are you willing to pay? It's important to research these things carefully.

"If the president of the United States, if he's smart, if he needs help, he'd come. I could do a favor for the president."

—*Paul Castellano*

LESSON

Never underestimate what you do for a living or what your stature or position could mean to someone else. Indeed the Roosevelt and Kennedy administrations had dealings with the mob. So did numerous other levels of state and city government at various times. Don't let anyone look down on you. No matter what you do for a living, do it with pride and use it to your best advantage when negotiating.

"I'm gonna make him an offer he can't refuse."

—*Don Corleone*

LESSON

Corleone's stratagy was based on hardball negotiating, Mafia-style. But Corleone was also known as a man who used the promises of friendship and rewards for favors granted to him. He was known for making business deals that had no appearance of heavy-handedness. However, being heavy-handed was not beyond him when it was required. In your business dealings, you wouldn't carry a gun to your office or to a meeting, but you can make an offer that gives your meeting partner something they either really want or need. How can you checkmate your associate into giving you what you want? Everybody has a price, so find out what that price is.

"Never get angry. Never make a threat. Reason with people."

—Don Corleone

LESSON

If you show anger in your business life, it will most likely be returned to you twofold. Threats usually enrage people rather than getting them to capitulate. Never make a threat unless you are ready to go all out. More often than not, a kind word works much better. Cooler heads always prevail in business, and reason is a good trump card to keep in your hand at all times.

"Never tell anybody outside the family what you're thinking again."

—Don Corleone

LESSON

Keep your own counsel at work. It's imperative that business strategies remain as secretive as possible. Such strategies should be shared within the corporation so that everyone is on the same page. But don't share them outside the company. Keep your strategic advantage for as long as possible.

POWER

"In this country, you gotta make the money first. Then when you get the money, you get the power. Then when you get the power, then you get the women."

—*Tony Montana,* Scarface

LESSON

Money only gets you into the game. Money does not equal power. How does one accumulate power? Money is one of the ways. Holding favors for other people is another. Powerful people like to pal around with other powerful people. Introductions to and from other powerful people usually help you attain a higher level in your professional life.

"Paulie may have moved slow, but it was only because Paulie didn't have to move for anybody."

—*Henry Hill,* Goodfellas

LESSON

People with power don't have to move fast. The people who work for them are the ones who have to move quickly.

"Don't carry a gun. It's nice to have them close by, but don't carry them. You might get arrested."

—*John Gotti*

LESSON

If you have to carry heat to impose your will, you are not in charge. Real power is conferred and carried by men who don't have to carry weapons. Like generals or politicians, successful executives don't need to continually make shows of power if they wield it properly. If you need to make shows of power too often, then there is something wrong, and people will begin to lose respect for you.

REALITY

> **"There are only murderers in this room! Michael—open your eyes! This is the life we chose, the life we lead. And there is only one guarantee: none of us will see heaven."**
>
> —*John Rooney*, The Road to Perdition

LESSON

Don't close your eyes to reality. See your business and the people in it for who they are and what they have accomplished. Don't look down on anyone. Respect and understand the who, what, and why of each situation you are dealing with.

RESPECT

"Those who want respect, give respect."

—*Tony Soprano*, The Sopranos

PROFILE

The Sopranos was an American television drama series created by David Chase. Set in New Jersey, the series revolves around mobster Tony Soprano and the difficulties he faces as he tries to balance the often conflicting requirements of his home life and the criminal organization he heads.

LESSON

Mutual respect goes a long way in business. If you don't respect your adversary—the competition, the marketplace, perhaps even a coworker—you may be unhappy with the end result. If you have no respect for other people, people in the end will have no respect for you.

RESPONSIBILITY

> "Do not allow anything into your life
> which you cannot walk out on
> in thirty seconds flat if you spot the heat
> around the corner."

—*Neil McCauley*, Heat

PROFILE

Neil McCauley is a criminal mastermind in Michael
Mann's 1995 thriller *Heat*. A Los Angeles crime saga,
Heat focuses on the lives of two men on opposite sides
of the law—one a detective (Al Pacino), the other a
thief (Robert De Niro).

LESSON

McCauley's motto is a simple one, but it requires
a lifetime of discipline and, ultimately, of solitude.
McCauley's motto means that attachments to things,
people, etc., can actually be encumbrances. For some
people encumbrances might come in the form of family,
pets, friends, a house, or a city or town. McCauley's
motto means that all of these things may keep you from
achieving your goal or from making a move in your
career when you have to.

RISK

> ## "He knew the risks, he didn't have to be there. It rains . . . you get wet."
>
> *—Neil McCauley*

LESSON

Don't lie to yourself. Always know what the risks are. Understand the odds before you do something. Take into account all aspects before taking a risk. No one will mourn your recklessness or your fate when you knowingly take a risk.

RULES

"**Rule number one: don't underestimate the other guy's greed. Rule number two: don't get high on your own supply.**"

—*Frank Lopez,* Scarface

LESSON

Frank Lopez's dictum is an important one. Never underestimate your enemy, whether in your own office or in the business world at large. And never get too entranced with your own product. Be realistic and always look at it for what it is (and isn't).

SATISFACTION

"**You know what, when we started out, I thought we was really goin' somewhere. This is it. We're just goin', huh?**"

—*Bonnie Parker*, Bonnie and Clyde

PROFILE

Arthur Penn's stunning 1967 crime drama, *Bonnie and Clyde*, is based on the real-life Great Depression–era bank robbers Bonnie Parker (October 1, 1910–May 23, 1934) and Clyde Barrow (March 24, 1909–May 23, 1934).

LESSON

Satisfaction is an elusive thing. It is different for each and every person. You need to figure out what satisfaction is for yourself and then pursue it.

SUPPLY AND DEMAND

"I am like any other man. All I do is supply a demand."

—*Al Capone*

LESSON

No matter what business you're in, it's all about supply and demand. Are you supplying something someone wants? Are you looking for ways to make it more desirable? What does your customer want? Are you supplying it well? Are you delivering on time? You can always do it better. If you can't, someone else will.

"If you have a lot of what people want and can't get, then you can supply the demand and shovel in the dough."

–Charlie "Lucky" Luciano

LESSON

What are people looking for from your line of work? Can you make it happen? Can you deliver it faster or better than your competition? How else can you make your product or service so that people will continue to want it? Remember, in business you always have to keep your supply one step ahead of the demand.

TALENT

"**The saddest thing in life is wasted talent, and the choices that you make will shape your life forever.**"

—*Calogero "C" Anello*, A Bronx Tale

PROFILE

Calogero Anello is the young boy growing up, admiring both his father and a local mobster. But in the end, both men have similar views on only one thing: Calogero. Both express with different words the same meaning—that Calogero is a bright, young man who will waste his life if he does not make better decisions.

LESSON

Everyone has a talent of some sort. The problem in this world is that some people have talents they are not utilizing. What is it that you do well? Are you doing it to the best of your ability? Are you living up to your potential? Are you working as hard as you can? Are you outperforming your coworkers? The competition? Be sure to give it your all every day in the workplace.

TEAMWORK

"Baseball! A man stands alone at the plate. This is the time for what? For individual achievement. There he stands alone. But in the field, what? Part of a team. Teamwork. . . . Looks, throws, catches, hustles. Part of one big team. Bats himself the live-long day, Babe Ruth, Ty Cobb, and so on. If his team don't field . . . what is he? You follow me? No one."

—*Al Capone*, The Untouchables

LESSON

Individual achievement is important, but teamwork carries the day. You need to do things so you shine at work, but they cannot come at the expense of the company or a coworker. Your accomplishments at the end of the day are only good as long as they serve the needs of the company. Anything else outside that doesn't count—and in some circumstances might be considered counterproductive. Don't just ask yourself how you can shine; ask how can you shine *and* serve the team.

"I'm a spoke on a wheel. I am, and so are you."

—"Lefty" Ruggiero

PROFILE

Benjamin "Lefty" Ruggiero was born on April 19, 1926, in New York City's Little Italy. He was a made member of the Bonanno crime family and a close friend/soldier under Dominic "Sonny Black" Napolitano. Mike Newell's 1997 movie *Donnie Brasco* tells the story of real-life FBI undercover agent Joe Pistone, who posed as jewel thief Donnie Brasco and who befriended Ruggiero.

LESSON

Everyone has to remember that everything doesn't revolve around them. No matter how important you are to the organization, the organization continues like a great wheel, and you're one of the parts. That is not a bad thing. It is what it is. It's about being a part of something, about being a team player. It's important that we all do our jobs, or the wheel doesn't roll and it all falls apart.

> **"You are no better or worse than anyone else in La Cosa Nostra. You are your own man. You and your father are now equals. Your father, sons, and brothers have no priority. We are all as one, united in blood. Once you become part of this, there is no greater bond."**
>
> *—Thomas DiBella*

PROFILE

Thomas DiBella was a captain in the Columbo crime family. After attempts were made on Colombo's life, leaving him in no position to run the family, the leadership fell to DiBella. He was a man adept at evading the authorities since his sole bootlegging conviction in 1932. DiBella stepped down due to ill health in 1977.

LESSON

The company is all. Your welfare and well being are not above the company's welfare and well being. In the natural order of things, the company's health is everything. You are part of an organization. Your job is to help make the organization run smoothly. That is each worker's job.

THREATS

"Are you gonna bark all day, little doggy, or are you gonna bite?"

—*Mr. Blonde,* Reservoir Dogs

PROFILE

Mr. Blonde was played by Michael Madsen in Quentin Tarantino's stunning 1992 directorial debut, *Reservoir Dogs*. The movie features a group of men dealing with a botched jewel heist as they try to figure out who among them is a traitor.

LESSON

Don't make threats. You put people on guard. You also prove, if you do not follow up, that you are not a person to be taken seriously.

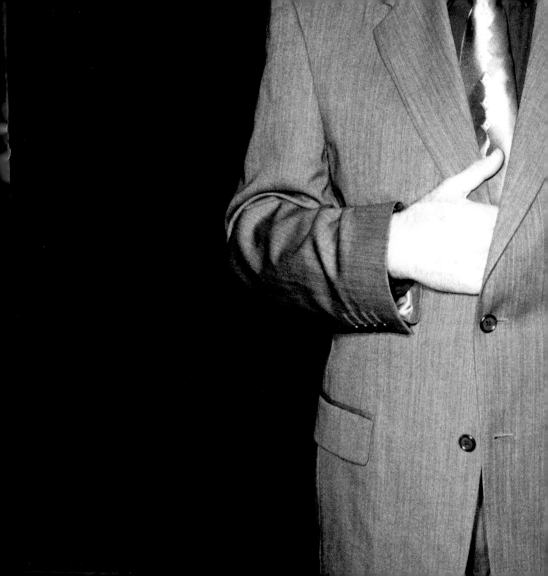

"You hear me talkin', hillbilly boy? I ain't through with you by a damn sight. I'ma get medieval on your ass."

—Marsellus Wallace

PROFILE

Marsellus Wallace, portrayed by Ving Rhames, is the crime kingpin of Los Angeles in Quentin Tarantino's masterpiece *Pulp Fiction*. Wallace is a tough crime lord, and his vengeance is powerful, painful, and ugly.

LESSON

Always make sure you haven't pissed someone off to the point where they are going to get retribution. Wallace's quote is a weird twist on Michiavelli: never do an enemy a small harm. So, be warned: when you attempt to take out a competitor or adversary and you fail, retribution could very well be medieval.

TRUST

"You heard of the double cross? In this business you gotta watch for the triple cross. You gotta always be alert. There's so much jealousy. Guys always trying to set you up, put you in traps. Trying to get ya killed. There was so much viciousness in this thing."

—*Nick Caramandi*

PROFILE

Nick Caramandi was a *guman* in the Scarfo crime family in Philadelphia.

LESSON

Success in business is not just about watching the people in the cubicles around you. It's also about watching your competitors. Sometimes it's the guy in third place that tries to take you out, not the guy who's in first. Always know everything about your competitors, whether they are in the executive suite or in the marketplace, and be very careful who you trust.

"In Vegas, everybody's gotta watch everybody else. Since the players are looking to beat the casino, the dealers are watching the players. The box men are watching the dealers. The floor men are watching the box men. The pit bosses are watching the floor men. The shift bosses are watching the pit bosses. The casino manager is watching the shift bosses. I'm watching the casino manager. And the eye-in-the-sky is watching us all."

—*Ace Rothstein*, Casino

LESSON

Trust in the workplace is a tricky thing. You want to trust everyone, and you want everyone to trust you. Yet trust is a fragile thing that can be easily destroyed by even the smallest of incidents or misunderstandings. Always assume you're being watched at work—your boss, your coworkers, even your customers are all keeping tabs on your performance and your level of honesty, integrity, and trustworthiness. And you should keep a sharp eye on those around you at the same time. Only through mutual verification of actions and intentions can trust be truly maintained in the workplace.

WARFARE

"Leave the gun, take the cannolis."

—*Pete Clemenza*, The Godfather

LESSON

Whether you're in the boardroom or fighting it out on the streets, remember to keep your head about you at all times. Remain calm and dispassionate. Do not let anger cloud your judgment. And remember to treat yourself and savor some of the sweet rewards that come with the job.

"Say hello to my little friends."

—*Tony Montana*, Scarface

LESSON

Life at work is filled with good and bad moments. Do you have the fortitude and firepower to face the bad times? If you are going to remain on the radar as a business or as an individual within a business, companies or people are going to try and knock you off. That's the way it is. If you live your life under the radar, like the old-time mobsters, you might make it unscathed, but generally in the end, we all need to face down a few enemies or difficult circumstances. At one point or another, life at work gets rough. Make sure you have the willpower and firepower to face down your enemies and difficult situations. Or *you* may end up sleeping with the fishes!

ABOUT THE AUTHOR

Carlo De Vito is a longtime publishing executive and is the author of *The Godfather Classic Quotes*, and the editor of *The International Encyclopedia of World Organized Crime*. He lives in Freehold, New Jersey, and Hudson, New York, with his wife, sons Dylan and Dawson, and their dogs.

ABOUT

CIDER MILL PRESS

Good ideas ripen with time. From seed to harvest, Cider Mill Press strives to bring fine reading, information, and entertainment together between the covers of its creatively crafted books. Our Cider Mill bears fruit twice a year, publishing a new crop of titles each spring and fall.

Visit us on the web at
www.cidermillpress.com
or write to us at
12 Port Farm Road
Kennebunkport, Maine 04046